T0117648

BRITAIN'S HERITAGE

Morris Minor

Gillian Bardsley

AMBERLEY

Acknowledgements

The author would like to thank Colin Corke, Tom Morley, Zac Ware, Lisa Hudman and Mollie Horne for their support in researching and preparing this book. All the images in this book are the copyright of the British Motor Industry Heritage Trust (BMIHT) with the following exceptions: p. 9 (top), the Issigonis Estate; p. 53 (top), p. 56 (top), p. 58 (bottom) and p. 62, Gillian Bardsley; p. 55, p. 60 and p. 61, Tom Morley; and p. 57, p. 58 (top) and p. 59, the Morris Minor Centre.

First published 2017

Amberley Publishing
The Hill, Stroud
Gloucestershire, GL5 4EP

www.amberley-books.com

Copyright © Gillian Bardsley, 2017

The right of Gillian Bardsley to be identified as the Author of this work has been asserted in accordance with the Copyrights, Designs and Patents Act 1988.

ISBN 978 1 4456 6898 7 (paperback)
ISBN 978 1 4456 6899 4 (ebook)

All rights reserved. No part of this book may be reprinted or reproduced or utilised in any form or by any electronic, mechanical or other means, now known or hereafter invented, including photocopying and recording, or in any information storage or retrieval system, without the permission in writing from the Publishers.

British Library Cataloguing in Publication Data.
A catalogue record for this book is available from the British Library.

Printed in the UK.

Contents

A two-door Morris Minor 1000 pictured in the grounds of Blenheim Palace in 1965.

1

Introduction: Morris Motors and the Rising Design Star

Though it was not the first to bear the name, the car that is universally acknowledged as *the* Morris Minor was launched in 1948 by Morris Motors. It was manufactured for twenty-three years and reached a total of 1.6 million before production ended in 1972.

The story of the Morris Minor is bound up with three men who each, in his own way, affected the course of the British motor industry. They were from different generations and at very different stages of their lives in 1940 when this story begins. Lord Nuffield, the founder of Morris Motors and a wealthy philanthropist, was looking towards his legacy as he neared retirement; his Vice-chairman, Miles Thomas, was at the mid-point of a distinguished managerial career; and the young designer, Alec Issigonis, was just beginning his path to fame.

The Austin Motor Company and Morris Motors were the two big rivals of the British motor industry in its early years. Herbert Austin, born in 1866, had entered the business

In 1903 William Morris went into business with two partners to open the Oxford Automobile and Cycle Agency. It proved a bitter experience, failing after only a year. Thereafter, Morris preferred to work alone.

early, building prototype cars in the 1890s before setting up the Austin Motor Company at Longbridge near Birmingham in 1905. This was a typical large-scale engineering plant where every part of the car was manufactured on site. William Morris, born a decade later in 1877, began his career as a cycle mechanic before becoming a garage owner involved in the repair, servicing and hire of cars. Though he set up a motor assembly business at Cowley on the outskirts of Oxford in 1913, the First World War brought his progress to a sharp halt. In 1919, when civilian production resumed, he restarted his business as Morris Motors with the Morris Oxford and Morris Cowley (also known as 'Bullnoses') as his main products. As a relative latecomer, Morris knew he could not afford the Austin approach to manufacturing, so he concentrated on assembly, allowing his supplier firms to carry the large overheads incurred in production of the component parts.

The 1920s was a period of deep recession. Austin got into severe financial difficulty with its post-war model programme, and the Austin Seven, launched in 1922, would be crucial to its survival. This was the first 'real' car to be designed on such a small scale and would dominate the small car market in Britain for the rest of the decade. Meanwhile, William Morris was doing well enough to begin taking over his suppliers and rival firms which had got in to difficulty. In 1927 Morris Motors ventured into direct competition with the Austin Seven by launching the first car to use the name 'Morris Minor'. A price-cutting war ensued, which reached its peak in 1931 when a Morris Minor two-seater tourer became the first car with a price tag of £100. This was a good publicity stunt, but it was still a lot of money for a very basic car and the Morris Minor would never be as popular or as versatile as its Austin rival.

The Morris Minor was a first attempt to compete with the Austin Seven. This illustration from 1933 demonstrates its usefulness for everyday tasks such as shopping, but it could not rise to the sporting success enjoyed by its rival.

There were other competitors, such as the American company Ford, the pioneers of mass-production methods enabling them to produce cheap cars. In 1933 they introduced the Ford 'Model Y' 8 hp saloon (or Ford Eight). This car, rather than the Morris Minor, became the main competition to the Austin Seven. In June 1935, a reduced specification model with four seats was the only closed-body car ever to sell in Britain for £100, a price it held until July 1937.

William Morris was a complicated man. At his core he was a hard-nosed businessman, self-conscious about his Oxfordshire accent, and determined to exceed the limitations of his modest background. By 1929 he had become Baron Nuffield and his expanding network of companies was operating as the Nuffield Organisation. Despite his growing wealth he chose to live comfortably rather than ostentatiously, giving much of his fortune away to philanthropic causes, which led to his elevation as Viscount Nuffield in 1938. As he grew older, however, his determination often manifested itself as intransigence, as he put his own instincts ahead of the advice of those he had appointed to look after his business for him.

Throughout the 1920s Nuffield relied on his close friend (and in due course his Vice-chairman) Leonard Lord, an abrasive man who was not well-liked by his colleagues. Lord successfully modernised the Nuffield factories using the principles pioneered by Ford. The product range was updated too, and the Morris Eight (a thinly disguised copy of the Ford Eight) replaced the Morris Minor in 1934. Austin's follow-up models had failed to capitalise on the dominance of the Seven, and the Morris Eight began to overtake it, especially when it was updated as the more powerful 'Series E' in 1938.

The attraction of pre-war small cars was to evade the tax that penalised engines larger than 8 hp. This is a Morris Eight Series E from 1938 – a stylish car that boasts a sliding roof.

Morris (left) understood the value of good publicity and hired Miles Thomas (right) to raise his company's profile. In a typical stunt from 1924, this Morris Oxford 'Bullnose' was driven from Land's End to John O'Groats without stopping the engine.

Leonard Lord did not stay to see the success of his endeavours. Having grown tired of Lord Nuffield's interference, he left the company in 1936 and joined Austin two years later. Hurt by this turn of events, Nuffield waited until 1940 before appointing a forty-three-year-old Welshman named Miles Thomas to the Vice-chairman position. Thomas had trained as an engineer but, after leaving the RAF at the conclusion of the First World War, he decided to try his hand as a journalist, reporting on motor races all over Europe from the cockpit of an aeroplane. William Morris was far ahead of his competitors in understanding the need for effective publicity and he persuaded Thomas to join the company to promote its products. Within a few years, Nuffield had promoted him to a managerial position until, finally, he was chosen for the most senior position in the company. His experience outside the motor industry gave him a different perspective and his pleasant personality meant he was able to exercise effective leadership without the bullying style of his predecessor, Len Lord.

The Second World War, which broke out in 1939, once again brought civilian car production to a complete halt. Miles Thomas skilfully managed the Nuffield Organisation's war effort and his achievements were officially recognised by the award of a knighthood in 1942. No civilian, however, was immune from the mundane duties imposed by constant air-raids. One night he found himself on the roof of the Cowley factory undertaking fire-watching duty. With him were his Chief Engineer, Vic Oak, and a junior member of Oak's team.

Above: Though the Austin Seven was meant to be a small family car, Alec Issigonis was one of many young men who converted them into sporting machines. His love of driving influenced the road-holding qualities he imbued in all his designs.

Below: Issigonis joined Morris Motors in 1936 and his first job was to work on a coil spring and wishbone independent front suspension with rack-and-pinion steering for the Morris Ten, which was the company's first attempt at a chassis-less car.

This introduces the third character in our story, a highly talented but as yet unproven young designer named Alec Issigonis. Born in 1906, Issigonis grew up in the coastal port of Smyrna, Turkey. His father was of Greek descent, his mother of German descent, but the family was lucky enough to have British citizenship, so when civil war broke out in 1922 they were rescued as part of an official evacuation carried out by the Royal Navy. The once-wealthy family became penniless refugees. His father died along the way, but Issigonis and his mother reached London in 1923 where he began his quest to follow in his father's footsteps and become an engineer. He joined Morris Motors in 1936, a junior draughtsman in the drawing office, and his first task was to work on a coil spring and wishbone independent front suspension with rack-and-pinion steering for the Morris Ten. Though the suspension was not used on the final version of the car, this was for reasons other than the quality of the engineering, and by 1938 Issigonis had achieved the status of Project Designer.

At this stage of his life, Issigonis was a mixture of diffidence and quiet self-confidence. His personal ambition was great, his determination fierce, but he was not yet in a position to achieve his dreams. In his spare time he channelled his energy into racing Austin Sevens, before moving on to build his own racing car, which was much admired and went by the name of the 'Lightweight Special'. Thomas recorded his first impression of him as 'a shy, reserved young man'; but fire-watching duty was not the most exciting of pursuits, and the Vice-chairman was soon able to encourage Issigonis to share his thoughts about his favourite subject – small car design.

2

Designing a Car for the Post-War Era

Alec Issigonis was not called up to the forces because engineering was a 'reserved' profession and officially his job was to design vehicles to help win the war. He would become famous for his technique of expressing ideas through freehand sketches that were artistic rather than technical. He began to sketch tanks, armoured cars and an 'amphibious' wheelbarrow which were all built and tested, though few of them made it to the front line. Miles Thomas, as Vice-chairman, was responsible for co-ordinating the company's war production. Neither of them, however, was entirely focussed on the military effort. Despite the ban placed on the production of cars for civilian use by the Ministry of Transport in October 1940, Thomas knew it was essential to plan for a post-war model range. He implemented a discreet development programme in 1941, codenamed 'Mosquito' after the famous de Havilland fighter bomber. It was part of a project to create a family of three related designs for a small, mid-sized, and large car.

He then suggested to his fire-watching companion that he could turn his inventive mind to the problem. Because of the need for secrecy, Issigonis began a second set of notebooks alongside his military designs, sketching ideas for the Mosquito at the dining room table of the modest Oxford flat he shared with his mother. By the end of 1943 the war was going sufficiently well for the Ministry of Transport to give car manufacturers permission to work

on designs and prototypes for post-war models, which meant that the hundreds of sketches already produced by Issigonis could finally be translated into a real working prototype for road-testing.

As the workload increased, Issigonis was allocated a small team to assist. Jack Daniels, with whom he had already formed a partnership before the war, returned to work on chassis and suspension. They were joined by body specialist Reginald Job. The team was allocated a small

A portrait of Alec Issigonis in 1938. He was just beginning to establish himself at Morris Motors, impressing his bosses with his commitment and ingenuity.

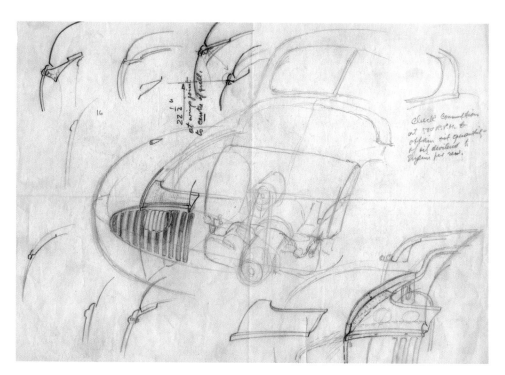

In the early 1940s, the Issigonis creativity was in full flow. This sketch shows the split windscreen and distinctive grille that would appear on earlier Mosquito prototypes, as well as the flat four engine that was later dropped.

The first full-sized prototype was built in 1944. This early version had a 6 hp engine and was painted in gun-metal grey. The factory walls behind are painted with wartime camouflage. You can see how similar it looks to the sketch above.

workshop away from the main office, with a few skilled mechanics to assist them. Secrecy was still paramount; Morris Motors could not appear to be diverting too much effort away from the war effort and also wished to keep its plans from the prying eyes of its competitors.

A small-scale 'cell' working on every aspect of the car was not a normal way of designing. It was more usual to use teams of specialists – Issigonis himself had originally been part of a team working on suspensions when he joined the company. Speaking to Philip Turner in 1978 Issigonis contemptuously compared 'modern' methods of design to his tight-knit team: '...we used to work like stink, we were so dedicated to it. Now, the world is just the other way round. Nobody can make a decision unless you have got twenty people at a meeting because they are afraid to do so.'

The Mosquito was not a revolutionary expression of previously unknown ideas. The genius of Issigonis throughout his career was to immerse himself in the best engineering available and combine different elements in a creative way. Among the models he studied were the Fiat 500 'Topolino' from Italy, the Citroën Traction Avant from France, and the Steyr from Germany. The features that caught his interest included a forward-mounted engine, independent front suspension, rack and pinion steering, lightweight bodywork, and unitary construction. Front-wheel drive was one idea he did not pursue. Issigonis would later say that the reason it did not appear on the Morris Minor was because, at that stage of his career, he could not find a way to make it work.

When he began the Mosquito project, Issigonis studied other contemporary designs. This early drawing of a two-seater echoes the lines of the German Steyr and the Fiat Topolino.

He was also looking at American cars, with their elegant styling. This picture of a Pontiac was taken at Cowley in 1939, showing that such cars were being evaluated by Morris Motors even before the war began.

Though the Mosquito would become the first British mass-market production car to incorporate these features, it did not look like any of them. He was also interested in perfecting the lines of the car to produce a pleasing aesthetic shape. His sketches began to echo the streamlining and curvature of American style, with the wings merging into the doors, the base of the body running as parallel as possible to the ground, and the absence of running boards. The Cowley negative archive confirms that the Experimental Department obtained examples of both a Pontiac and a Chevrolet that Issigonis would have studied, not just for their style but also to learn about their underlying structure. The result was a strong visual statement in contrast to the upright and 'boxy' shape typical of pre-war British designs.

Another of his preoccupations was space utilisation. The unusual engine position allowed for a shortened bonnet which in turn allowed a lengthening of the passenger space. Special 14-inch wheels, manufactured by Dunlop, were the smallest wheels designed to that date, helping to lower the car's centre of gravity and reducing unsprung weight, which contributed to good road-holding and a comfortable ride. They also took up less room, thus assisting in his quest for a roomy interior.

Issigonis liked to do his own prototype testing in order to assess the strengths and weaknesses of a design. At the end of 1944 he set off on an extended run from Cowley to North Wales. The flat four engine that was under development was not sufficiently advanced, so a side-valve engine as used by the Morris Eight was fitted for testing purposes. Though, when he became famous, Issigonis would say that he did not care about the opinions of ordinary people when he was designing a car, the report he presented to the senior management shows a keen interest in the reactions of passers-by. 'The car attracts an almost embarrassing degree of attention' he wrote, 'particularly when passing through towns. It was noted that this was not confined to the younger sections of the population. Comment from people who actually had an opportunity of examining the car was 99 per cent favourable.' There were

Issigonis testing a prototype in October 1946. The car now has the 'headlamps in the grille' configuration with which it would go to market.

few cars on the road during the war, not just because they were limited to essential use, but also because of petrol shortages, so this is hardly surprising.

The war in Europe reached a conclusion at the end of 1945 and British motor manufacturers were now free to put their pre-war models back into production until they had something else ready. Up to this point, the Miles Thomas plan, ably executed by Issigonis and his team, seemed to be going along nicely. The Morris Eight Series E returned to the assembly hall, while the Mosquito project gathered pace. Six prototypes were commissioned and Reg Job started to prepare the body drawings for assembly. The objective was to launch the car at the end of 1947. This is when Lord Nuffield returned to the story, and not in a helpful way. His reaction to the Mosquito was instant dislike, referring to it as 'the poached egg'. He protested to his Vice-chairman that the factory already had more orders for the Morris Eight than it could fulfil, so where was the need for something so unconventional? Miles Thomas patiently explained that this was simply a result of excessive demand: '...anybody who wanted [a car] put in an order for at least five different makes, and when one of them was delivered the other four orders were not worth the paper they were written on'. Lord Nuffield refused to believe him

Did you know?

The Morris Minor design included a starting handle – a traditional device that made it possible to start a car when the battery was not charged. This remained right until the end of production in 1972 and was cited by the police as a bonus point when choosing it for patrol duty.

Above: After the war finished the factory could start tooling up to put the car into production. This bodyshell from 1946 demonstrates the unitary construction, which was a pioneering technique for a car of this size.

Below: Early brochures emphasised the importance of space utilisation. Accommodating the passenger compartment within the wheelbase, it was explained, created comfort, stability and easy driving.

 ALL PASSENGERS SIT INSIDE THE WHEELBASE—THAT'S WHY THE

MORRIS MINOR IS *Supreme in Comfort—*

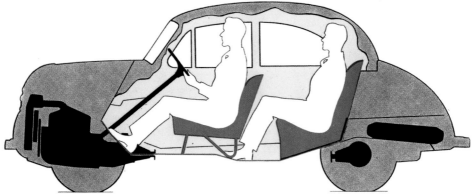

The interior of the production car in 1948. The symmetrical dashboard layout includes a speedometer on the right with either a Morris badge (as in this picture) or optional clock on the left. Underneath is an open parcel shelf.

and insisted that a bit of restyling and the addition of the Mosquito suspension to the Morris Eight was all that was needed. Vic Oak's department dutifully built a prototype to Nuffield's suggested specification, but it was concluded that the tooling costs would be prohibitive and the timescale of a launch in the spring of 1949 unattainable. Meanwhile, competitors were getting on with the job. While Nuffield argued with his Vice-chairman, Austin (now under the leadership of Leonard Lord) began to sell the Austin A40 range in 1947 – an all-new mid-sized saloon with 1,200cc engine and American-influenced styling.

Issigonis left the board politics to his mentor. Pondering over the proportions of the final prototype, he went back to the workshop with his mechanics and asked them to cut the bodyshell in half. Then he asked them to move the pieces apart and back together, finally making the judgement that the car needed an extra four inches down the middle. With this simple action, Issigonis managed to turn the obstacle of Nuffield's opposition into an opportunity to improve his design. The wider frame provided more stability, giving better handling; it increased the interior space he was so keen on; and, in contrast to the narrowness of pre-war designs, it created a 'modern' look that helped the car to age better than many of its contemporaries.

After seeing the widened version in late 1947, Miles Thomas decided he could not allow Lord Nuffield to continue with his blocking tactics. To remove any further excuse for delay, he stopped work on development of the flat four engine, substituting the existing sidevalve

Above: Sir Miles Thomas in his office in 1944 using a dictating machine. The Mosquito project might never have become a reality without his determined support in the face of Lord Nuffield's intransigence.

Below: The Morris Minor went into production in 1948. The consequence of widening of the body is evident from the flat panel in the middle of the bonnet and the joining bridge in the front bumper.

Lord Nuffield could not summon up any enthusiasm for the Morris Minor. He stares gloomily into the engine bay in October 1948. At this stage only a handful of cars had been completed in preparation for the launch.

unit from the Morris Eight, which had been used in prototype tests. The change of engine required little adjustment to the engineering of the car, so Jack Daniels did not have a problem with it. It was body engineer Reg Job who had to fit the extra four inches into the bodyshell. He could not start again because much of the body-tooling was already complete. Instead, he created a flat area in the centre of the car where the join occurred and inserted metal strips in to the floor pan, avoiding the need to alter the overall layout. There was one thing it was too late to change – the only way of stretching out the front and rear bumpers was to add a metal bridge in the middle. This would create an unintentional but distinctive feature of the early production cars.

Once the specification was fixed, Thomas went back to Lord Nuffield and insisted that a date must be set for the end of Morris Eight production. Getting the Mosquito out of the experimental shop and onto the production line was his last action at the Nuffield Organisation. Like Leonard Lord before him, he had grown tired of fighting Lord Nuffield, and he left the company at the end of 1947 to take up new challenges outside the motor industry.

Did you know?

Despite his dislike of the Morris Minor, even Lord Nuffield could not escape the reality of the car's success. In 1957 the Nuffield Organisation presented him with a gold-plated silver model of the car to celebrate his 80th birthday. Possibly, they had not consulted him about his preferred gift.

3
A Small Car Interpretation of a Big Car Specification

Reginald Hanks, the new Vice-chairman, quickly took the baton, ensuring that there were no further interruptions to the momentum that had built up behind the Mosquito project. In December 1947 it was decided that the smallest car in the new model range would be given the more conventional name of 'Morris Minor', harking back to the first small Morris car of the pre-war era. If this was an attempt to mollify Lord Nuffield it was not successful, as he refused to drive the car for publicity photographs. Also ready for launch were the Morris Oxford and Six, which were six-seaters, and the Wolseley 4/50 and 6/80, which had a more luxurious trim. These larger cars were similar to the Minor in appearance.

The first London Motor Show for ten years was imminent – a perfect launchpad for the post-war motor industry. It was held at Earls Court between 27 October and 6 November 1948 and attracted a record attendance of over half a million compared to a previous best of less than a quarter of a million. The crowds were not disappointed. The sports car category

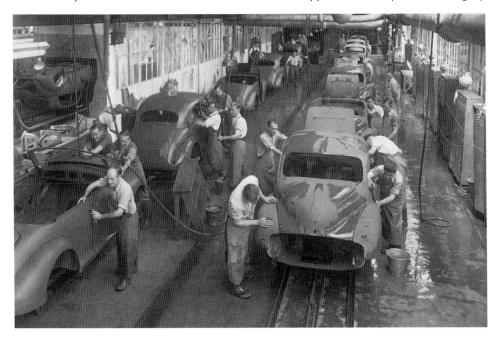

By 1949 the car had finally reached the production line. On the main track, bodies are being rubbed down. On the left the unitary construction can be seen in the bodyshell being hoisted on its roof into the paint booth.

featured the Jaguar XK120 and the Bristol 401. There was an early version of the Land Rover – a seven-seat station wagon with a Tickford body. In the family class were a brand new Hillman Minx, the Austin A70 Hampshire, plus the Vauxhall Velox and Wyvern. Some cars such as the Austin A90 Atlantic were designed specifically to target the North American market.

Now that the arguments were concluded, Morris Motors was able to take its place on Stand 163 between Rolls-Royce and Vauxhall. For once the delay played in its favour, as it was able to withhold details of the new cars in advance, thus creating an extra buzz around the stand. *Motor Sport*'s show preview could only say: 'The 1949 Morris models are being kept secret until today. We believe an aerodynamic car with the four-cylinder side-valve engine used in the former 'Eight' will be on show, together with larger models, one of which will be called the Morris Oxford. Go and see for yourselves!'

The car was launched at the 1948 Motor Show at the end of October. It was the mid-sized Oxford rather than the 'small' Minor that received the star billing. Interestingly, the artist has ignored the bumper's bridging piece.

Most manufacturers had chosen to showcase their larger models which was a logical move. At home, the RAC horsepower tax (first imposed in 1921) had just been replaced by a flat rate of £10 per car, which took away the price advantage of a small car, while larger cars had always been more popular in markets such as the USA. Morris Motors was no exception, putting the Morris Oxford at the front of the stand. Journalists and public alike, however, were more interested in the Morris Minor, which was represented by a saloon and also the more glamorous 'tourer' version. Visitors were attracted to its striking American styling influence, which made it seem modern and even a bit exotic in post-war austerity Britain. The press, who had the privilege of trying it out, were full of praise for its superior handling, innovative suspension, and exceptional space utilisation.

Did you know?

In 1952 a company called Airflow Streamlines offered to convert the tourer to a saloon for £85 in seven days, claiming this would increase the value of the car by £100, thus providing the owner with a small profit. In recent years, it has become popular to convert saloons back to convertibles.

This tourer from 1949 has landed in one of the more glamorous destinations, Curaçao island in South America. It still had the 'headlamps in the grille' configuration that Issigonis had designed.

The Autocar called it 'a triumph in good looks'. *The Motor* proclaimed: 'Among the record number of visitors to the Earls Court motor exhibition last October there were many who felt that the new Morris Minor "Stole the Show"... There can be no pretence that it approaches perfection, but it is a car which pleases both driver and passengers and which will almost exactly fulfil the requirement of tens of thousands of motorists in this country and abroad – there has been nothing like it in the economy car class previously.'

In the next few years rival firms would do their best, but none could match the inherent qualities of the Morris Minor either in external elegance or underlying engineering. As a result, unlike its predecessors such as the Austin Seven and the pre-war Morris Minor, it was a small car that was attractive in its own right and not just something for people who couldn't afford anything else. At the end of a road test published in February 1949, *The Motor* made this very point:

> The highest tribute to the Minor is that a variety of drivers hitherto enthusing over larger and faster cars suddenly began to feel that this grown-up baby could fulfil all their requirements and double their mpg figures. The real lament is that, ideally suited though it is to home needs, most of the new Minors will obviously go to keen buyers abroad.

Above: This transporter bears the words 'Nuffield Exports to the World'. Morris Minor tourers are being loaded onto a transporter headed for the docks and overseas markets.

Right: The cover of *Motoring* in 1953 celebrates 'Petrol Emancipation'. Instead of one type of low-grade fuel, this lucky Morris Minor owner now had a bewildering choice, each brand making big promises about its miraculous effects on his engine.

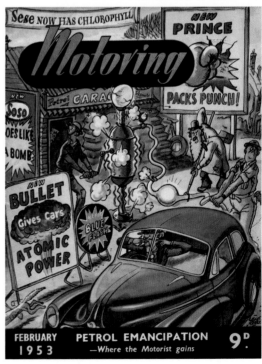

This was also true. By 1947 the Labour Government had decreed that 75 per cent of car production must go for export to bring much-needed foreign currency into an economy that had been badly damaged by five years of deadly attrition. Steel was rationed according to the ability of manufacturers to sell abroad. Punitive purchase taxes were reinforced by a 'covenant' that compelled those who bought a new car to keep it for at least a year. Thus, anyone who could afford a car (and this was still a minority in 1948) would have to satisfy themselves with a second-hand pre-war model for the time being. This was not the only thing home buyers had to contend with; throughout the war, petrol had not just been rationed, it was sold unbranded and 'pooled' to produce a single low-grade fuel. Rationing continued until March 1950 while pool petrol was not discontinued until 1953.

In its first twelve years of production, nearly half a million Morris Minors (48 per cent of the total manufactured) were sold abroad, with Australia as the top destination, followed by the USA. This led to the first major modification – raising the headlamps to comply with US safety regulations. Cars for all markets, including the UK, would adopt this change by January 1951. This was symptomatic of the continual delays that meant that, however good the Minor was in comparison to its competition, it was continually on the back foot. It was not easy to fit a heater with the side-valve engine – not a strong selling point when much of North America and Canada suffered from severe winter weather. It took too long to get production to the levels required to meet demand, while a patchy dealer network made it difficult for overseas customers to get spare parts. Many countries also had regulations stipulating that a percentage of the content must be locally sourced. This was addressed by setting up assembly plants abroad and many exports left Britain as 'Complete Knock Down' or CKD kits, to be assembled in Europe, Australia, and South Africa.

These cars are lined up outside the J. S. Inskip showroom for the launch of the Morris Minor in New York in 1949. Due to US safety regulations, the lamps had to be raised to the wings.

The new configuration improved visibility even if it displeased Issigonis. In 1951 the lighting units are undergoing a beam test in the factory to check their alignment. The bumper is now a single piece and the centre 'bridge" has disappeared.

Despite the export drive, the British economy was slow to recover during the 1950s. As the motor industry continued to struggle, the two bitter pre-war rivals would have little alternative but to join together. In 1952 it was announced that the Austin Motor Company and the Nuffield Organisation had agreed to merge as the British Motor Corporation (BMC). The death of Lord Austin in 1941 had cleared the way for Leonard Lord to take charge at Longbridge. He now gained control of the new Corporation and it was not long before Lord Nuffield retired to his country home of Nuffield Place in Oxfordshire.

This change would have big implications for the future of the Morris Minor and its creator Alec Issigonis. The success of his first design had naturally been good for his career, earning

Below left: Issigonis and his team were working on the new model range when he left in 1952. This sketch illustrates the new Morris Oxford. He intended the Minor to be a scaled-down version of the same shape.
Below right: A styling model for a redesigned Morris Minor was built, but BMC decided against making such a radical change to the appearance of one of its most popular models.

him promotion to Chief Engineer of Morris Motors in 1949. Following the merger he decided to leave the company for a new role at Alvis, sensing that a period of internal conflict lay ahead. Issigonis and his team had already begun work on the next generation of cars to succeed the 1948 model range, and though he was absent, his influence remained on the thinking of his former colleagues. One of the first new models launched in the BMC era was a completely restyled Morris Oxford Series II. A year later the Morris Six was replaced by the Morris Isis. Issigonis had always seen these three cars as part of a family and was never sentimental about updating his designs, however popular they might be. He had, therefore, also initiated work on a new Morris Minor whose body style would be a scaled down version of the Morris Oxford Series II. Leonard Lord, however, recognised that the Minor was one of the best and most recognisable cars of the combined Austin/Morris model range, so he saw no reason for drastic alterations.

As a result, from this point onwards the Minor would follow a different development path from its relatives. In 1952 the Morris Minor Series II was introduced. The styling was unchanged – indeed it was very hard to distinguish from the Series MM visually except for the smallest details. The most significant modification was the replacement of the pre-war side-valve engine. Morris Motors had already been working on a scheme to substitute the overhead-valve engine used by the Wolseley Eight, but Leonard Lord ditched this plan, much to the annoyance of the Cowley engineers. Instead, the Morris Minor was fitted with the overhead-valve 803cc A-series engine, which had made its first appearance in the Austin A30. In due course, the rear axle was also replaced. These changes improved the driveability of the car (and made it easier to install a heater) but they didn't make it faster because the A-series wasn't any more powerful than the engine it replaced and the car was 'under geared'. As *The Autocar* observed in a road test: 'Performance tests show that

The Morris Minor retained its distinctive shape, but was fitted with an A-Series engine. Relaunched as the Series II, this beautifully sectioned vehicle was displayed at the 1953 Motor Show, illustrating the space utilisation which was still a key selling-point.

A Morris Minor Series II in 1956. A recent facelift had introduced a slatted grille; the duotone colour scheme was never offered as standard. It was four years since the BMC merger but this showroom only contains Nuffield products.

the maximum speed is little changed, the latest car showing an improvement of 1 mph in the mean figures,' which could be interpreted as damning with faint praise. The early version came to be known as the 'cheesegrater' to distinguish it from the facelifted version, introduced two years later in 1954. This had a redesigned slatted grille that lasted until the end of production. There were also new seats and an updated dashboard with a central speedometer.

The benefit of the new engine was not properly unlocked until the introduction of the Morris Minor 1000 that, fittingly, made its first appearance at the 1956 Earls Court Motor Show. The engine size was increased to 948cc, complemented by some basic styling improvements. The split windscreen was replaced with a one-piece windscreen that was less prone to water leaks and had better visibility in rain. There was a wider rear window on the saloon, a remote-control gearchange and an upgraded interior – all offered without a price increase. This was more like it and sales improved at home and abroad. 1956 was also the year of the Suez crisis that for a short time led to renewed petrol rationing, and once again drivers were looking for a good, small car which was economical on fuel. There was even a brief revival in exports to the USA. The Suez crisis also affected North America, leading to a demand for 'compact cars'. As ever, BMC failed to take full advantage of this development, unable to supply the quantity requested by its US dealers or solve

Above: The Morris Minor 1000 followed in 1956. The body was modernised with a one-piece windscreen and enlarged back window, but the real difference lay under the bonnet with a more powerful engine.

Below: The Suez crisis of 1956 created a fuel shortage that was good for small cars such as the Morris Minor. Once again it was being promoted for its economical upkeep costs.

Above: The Morris Minor 1000 four-door in 1957. The centre pillar is still fitted with the semaphore 'swing out' trafficator system which was becoming increasingly dated as the 1950s progressed.
Below: A mock-up of 'XC9003' was compared to a Morris Minor at Longbridge in 1957. Just as the shape of the Mosquito emerged early in the design, so the future Mini already has its distinctive shape, despite being two years from launch.

The Morris Minor became the first British car to reach the remarkable production landmark of one million. BMC decided to push the boat out by bringing out a special edition, which was painted a distinctive lilac colour.

Issigonis had returned to BMC in 1955, so he was on hand to break a bottle of champagne across the bumper of a Morris Minor Million at the official celebrations in December 1960.

Did you know?

The limited edition Millionth Morris Minor had a special badge on the wing and bootlid that read – 'Minor 1000000'. This was created by the simple expedient of joining together two Minor '1000' badges with the middle '1' removed.

the problems with its dealer network, so the surge in exports foundered when conditions returned to normal.

This time the press were united in their praise. Jerry Ames of *Autocourse* spoke for many in expressing his surprise at the rejuvenation of an eight-year-old design:

> Some drivers will have the shock of their lives when they see a perfectly innocent looking small family saloon scoot rapidly past them. There won't be a thing they can do about it, unless they are driving something powerful, for keeping the new Morris Minor 1000 in sight over winding roads will need the skill of a Fangio or Moss... The old Minor had almost supernatural road-holding, but the latest version now adds real speed and acceleration to match... This car is definitely streets ahead of any other model of its type – be it British or Continental.

The Morris Minor 1000 quickly lifted home sales. At last, post-war austerity was easing, the cost of motoring was falling, and so more cars were making their way into the hands of the private British motorist. Many of the men who had been called up between 1939 and 1945 had been taught to drive during their military service. Women too (including heir apparent Princess Elizabeth) had been taught to drive tractors, lorries and buses while their men were away. Advertising for the original Morris Minor had emphasised its 'performance', 'economy' and 'comfort', but for the Morris 1000 the theme shifted, stressing the pleasure and freedom it could afford the whole family.

In the midst of these developments, Issigonis had re-joined BMC at the end of 1955. He began work on a whole new model range, which by 1959 had resulted in a fresh small car design that would become known as the Mini. Once again, it was a car which would steal the limelight because of its unconventional style and advanced technology. This could not, however, detract from the continuing success of his first design. At the end of 1960, the Morris Minor became the first British vehicle to reach the impressive landmark of one million sales and it was Issigonis who officiated at the celebrations on 22 December. The achievement was marked by the 'Morris Minor Million', with a fixed production of 350. This was an early example of a limited edition, painted in a distinctive lilac colour with ivory leather seats and black carpets. Although some continental marques had already reached bigger numbers, the fact was that their restricted model ranges made it a much easier goal for them to achieve. BMC, with its 'badge-engineering' policy and multiplicity of models, found it far more difficult to hit such targets.

4
Versatile and Useful

The Morris Minor was built for performance and a great deal of early publicity focussed on this aspect. One of the first publicity stunts saw a Morris Minor undertake a 1,600-mile round-trip from Calais through France to Monte Carlo. This car would later be recognised as the first and oldest Morris Minor in existence, with chassis number 501. A report of the journey, which appeared in *The Autocar* in February 1949, begins with a comment that illustrates the context of the times: 'The run begins amid the devastation caused by the war at the Calais docks.' The journalist soon moves on, however, to a more cheerful conclusion: 'The Morris Minor appeals because it is such a stout hearted, friendly little car; it goes fast and keeps on going.' Another notable example was a 3,000-mile round-trip undertaken in 1953 by two Morris Minor saloons across the Alaskan Highway, which was filmed by the Nuffield Cine Unit. Throughout the 1950s there were constant magazine reports of these and similar expeditions, official and unofficial, and across every continent.

The Cine Unit also recorded an ambitious record-breaking attempt at the Goodwood racing circuit in December 1952. The newly launched Morris Minor Series II, now fitted with an

The first Morris Minors were used as press cars. The car which would later be officially recognised as Morris Minor number one was sent on a 1,600-mile promotional trip from Calais to Monte Carlo in early 1949.

A battered grille testifies to the tough journey this car has endured from Delhi to London in 1956. The Nuffield Organisation was always happy to acknowledge such exploits, which demonstrated the quality of their products at no cost to themselves.

A-Series engine, was to undertake a non-stop 10,000-mile trial that required nine days and eight hours of continuous running at an average speed of 45 mph. The means of achieving this constituted a modern-day health and safety nightmare. At regular intervals, a special tender pulled by a Morris Oxford joined the track. The Morris Minor was then driven onto the back of the moving tender where it was secured by various locking pins and rods. The driving crew could now change over, while engineers quickly performed essential maintenance tasks such as refuelling, changing the wheels and oil, and taking readings of the car's performance, all without stopping the engine or the forward drive of the car. Finally, the tender would slow down, the car was released from its clamps, and the next driver would hang on as the Morris Minor bumped back onto the track to carry on under its own power for a few more hours.

The Series II looked much like the Series MM. The key difference was the A-Series engine, and in order to prove its qualities, BMC subjected it to a 10,000-mile non-stop trial over ten days at the Goodwood race track.

An early Morris Minor performed well in the 1949 Monte Carlo Rally. The car was invited to the factory where Vice-chairman Reginald Hanks personally congratulated (left to right) Betty Haig, Elsie Wisdom and Barbara Marshall on their achievement.

Did you know?

When the production milestone of one million was reached, BMC launched an appeal to find the oldest post-war Minor with 100,000 miles on the clock. After some deliberation over the eligibility criteria, the winner was announced as Mr Cyril Swift of Sheffield who was given a Morris Minor Million in exchange. Their discovery turned out to be NWL 576, the press car with chassis number 501 that had undertaken the Monte Carlo trip twelve years earlier.

The Morris Minor also enjoyed a brief career in motor sport, which has been rather overshadowed by the dominance of the Mini in racing and rallying during the 1960s. As early as January 1949, a Morris Minor with the registration NWL 858 was entered into the famous Monte Carlo Rally. The lead driver, Elsie Wisdom, was married to another successful rally driver, Tommy Wisdom. Betty Haig and Barbara Marshall completed her team. The race was described in detail by *Motor Sport* in March 1949 and the writer seemed a little taken aback by the result: 'The Monte Carlo Rally, held last month for the first time since the war, was a great success, and a gruelling test of the modern car which warranted, and received, world-wide publicity... The Morris Minor (1949 Minor we again emphasise!) was third in the 750 to 1,100-cc category.'

In addition, the Wisdom-Haig-Marshall team finished 47th overall out of 166 finishers and came second in the Ladies' Cup. Elsie's husband was driving with Donald Healey and Norman Black, but according to *Motor Sport* their day was less glorious: '...their Healey encountered blazing lorries blocking the ice-covered road en route for Milan, and losing marks for being late, they retired'. Betty Haig gave a vivid account of the experience: 'I think that the chief impression of the Monte Carlo Rally for anyone in the Morris Minor was of hard work! Constant time-checking on three stopwatch-clocks to keep up to the high set average without overdriving the little car, and never considering that we had any time in hand until actually within sight of the control!'

Car manufacturers considered motor sport to be an excellent way of showcasing the merits of their products. It was also an arena where women could compete on a level playing field with men. In 1955 the BMC Competitions Department was set up under the leadership of Marcus Chambers with a mission to race and rally cars from the entire model range, not just the more obvious sports versions. Two of his most important recruits were Pat Moss and Ann Wisdom, who had already formed a driving partnership at national rally level. Pat Moss was the younger sister of Stirling Moss and began competing in 1953 aged eighteen, driving her Morris Minor Convertible before buying a Triumph TR2. Ann Wisdom was the daughter of the very same Elsie who had done so well at Monte Carlo back in 1949. They would become a formidable partnership within the BMC Competitions Department and one of the first cars they were given was a Morris Minor 1000 with the registration NMO 933, nicknamed *Granny*

Pat Moss demonstrating her favourite car *Granny* to an enthralled crowd. She drove this Morris Minor in rallies between 1957 and 1960, gaining some notable results.

Ann Wisdom and Pat Moss in 1961. One of the Works team's strongest partnerships, their earliest success came a Morris Minor. They would go on to score the first rally victory for a Mini Cooper in the 1962 Tulip Rally.

by the team because of its durability. Pat Moss wrote enthusiastically about this car in her autobiography, which was published in 1967:

> The most fantastic, incredible car I have ever driven came into my hands in 1957. I am sure there has never been another like it – certainly I have never heard of one. I started driving it in rallies that year and four years later I was still driving it in rallies, long after other competition cars of its year had fallen to pieces or been pensioned off... It seemed to be unbreakable and the only time it did not finish was when I hit a big concrete post, and the poor thing could hardly be blamed for that. BMC kept wanting to give me a new car in its place, but I always asked for the same one again...

This was high praise from someone who would become famous for her stunning drives in Austin Healeys and Mini Coopers. To prove the point, an early test for *Granny* and BMC's new recruits was to be the four-day 'Marathon de la Route' of 1957 – one of the season's most difficult events. Marcus Chambers did not expect much of either the humble Morris Minor or its women drivers. Pat Moss recalled: 'he estimated that in *Granny* we would be late practically everywhere and ... if we found it all too much we should stop and they would not think any the worse of us as we were young and inexperienced', which, of course, was

A 'tourer' or open-top version was always part of the plan, and this prototype dates from 1947, before the bodyshell was widened.

NO PRICE PENALTY ON CONVERTIBLES ! You pay the same low price as for the sedan—actually hundreds of dollars under other makes.

There was some dithering over terminology for the open-top version and this North American brochure from 1949 boasts there is 'no price penalty on convertibles'. The illustration is meant to show how easy it is to assemble the canvas roof.

entirely the wrong thing to say to people as competitive as Moss and Wisdom. Not only did they finish, they came 23rd overall, fourth in their class, and second to an MGA in the Ladies' Cup. In the 1958 RAC Rally they did even better. *Granny* took fourth place overall, came first in the 1,000 cc Touring car class and won the Ladies' Cup. This was not only a personal best for Moss and Wisdom, it was also the BMC team's best rally result to date.

This sporting success was proof that the Morris Minor was more than just an economical small car with interesting styling. Throughout the 1950s, its strengths were built upon to produce a wide range of body styles that exploited the soundness and flexibility of the basic design. It had always been part of the plan to produce a soft-top version and a prototype 'tourer' was built as early as 1947, before the Mosquito body was widened. It was launched alongside the saloon at the 1948 Motor Show. Unlike other 'sporty' cars, the hood was much more than a flimsy screen against light rain. It was made of buff canvas fitted onto a semi-rigid frame that folded neatly on top of the boot when the car was open. When required, it was easy to manoeuvre into place – contemporary advertising made this point with its usual subtlety by regularly featuring the operation being undertaken by a woman. Weather-proofing was provided by winding glass windows at the front of the car and removable rear sidescreens that could be stowed in a canvas carrier in the boot when not needed. In 1951 the sidescreens were replaced by integrated glass rear windows and the rather old-fashioned term 'tourer' was dropped in favour of 'convertible'.

Even though BMC avoided making any fundamental changes to the Minor, other than replacing the side-valve engine, they were keen to diversify the options available in order to extend its appeal. In May 1953, the van (known as the quarter ton) and pick-up were launched. Over the next two decades these variants would become a ubiquitous sight on

Above: By 1954, when this Empire Green Series II model was made, the name had been officially changed from 'tourer' to 'convertible' and the removable rear sidescreens had been replaced with a fixed glass pane.

Below: The Morris Minor was notable for its unitary construction, but this had to be modified to build commercial and estate versions. This picture from 1951 shows a front compartment adapted so it can be fitted with alternative coachwork.

Above: This van carries the livery of Mills & Rockleys, a company specialising in billboard advertising. Some popular products from 1954 feature – Tide and Daz washing powder, Walls ice cream, Nestle milk and BSA motorbikes.

Below: A transporter leaving Cowley in 1961 carries an impressive group of Morris Minor commercials. Two quarter ton vans in Post Office and Royal Mail livery sit on either side of a Mini van. Underneath are two pickups.

The 'Traveller' was introduced in 1953. The farm setting seems to suggest it is an ideal utility vehicle, though compared to the van it would become more popular as a traditional estate car.

The Cowley assembly hall c. 1956. At the front of the picture is a Morris Minor 1000 Traveller with a BMC sticker in the windscreen. It is surrounded by Morris Oxford Series III saloons.

British roads. Numerous local shopkeepers, builders and traders adopted them as practical and economical vehicles for transport and delivery that could be customised with individual colours and liveries. They became popular with many of the national utility companies. One of the most interesting examples could be found at the Morris Motors factory in Cowley in the shape of a bright red fire engine, fully equipped with a comprehensive range of fire-fighting equipment. This special pickup was built in 1953 using the prototype chassis of the quarter ton van, and it was kept on active service until 1983.

In October 1953 an estate version, which would become known as the Morris Minor 'Traveller', joined the model range. Estates were commonly created by adding some additional passenger accommodation to an existing van. BMC took a different approach, starting instead with the passenger compartment, then adding the carrying capacity rather than the other way around. The Traveller was trimmed to the same standard as the saloon and included a rear bench seat with arm rests. The generous luggage compartment was easy to access through double doors at the back and the rear seats could be folded down to provide extra space. The finishing touch was large windows giving good all-round visibility. It was given a boost almost as soon as it was launched when new legislation enabled BMC to classify it as non-commercial, which removed lot of restrictions for its drivers, in particular a speed limit of 30 mph.

Did you know?

In the 1950s there were a number of different names for what we would now call an estate car. The rather colourful 'shooting brake' was a popular term in Edwardian times, while Austin would adopt the term 'countryman'. In early publicity the Morris Minors were referred to as station wagons (an American term). This was later changed to 'travellers cars', finally shortened to Traveller.

It was a very good-looking vehicle with a coachbuilt ash-frame body that gave it a sort of rural 'English' charm. The Englishness was something of an illusion – an earlier but notable example of this style was the American Ford V8 'Woodie' of the 1930s. The wooden structure was also problematic because it harked back to an earlier era of coachbuilding, carrying with it all the disadvantages of labour-intensive production methods that had been dispensed with during the 1920s by the introduction of the pressed-steel panel. Issigonis tried to reduce the manufacturing cost by using painted aluminium panels that fitted inside the wooden frame, but even so the structure was made up of fifty separate pieces of wood. As time went on, it would become one of the few vehicles on the road capable of failing its MOT as a result of wood rot. As was so often the case with BMC, a good original idea translated into a weakness, as rival manufacturers began to fabricate similar vehicles using a cheaper all-steel body.

The verdict of *Autocar* in June 1958 was, overall, a positive one:

Where the Traveller scores is in the successful merging of the willing work-horse with the Minor's well-liked attributes – economy, and handling qualities that are above average ... for the extra sum asked for this version of the Minor, not only is there greater usefulness and convenience, but the owner enjoys a standard of body appointment and finish which is superior to that of most cars of comparable size, and perhaps unequalled among small estate cars.

The Traveller's wooden frame was built at the Bodies Branch in Coventry using old coachbuilding methods. Once assembled they had to be loaded, with some difficulty, onto transporters, so they could be united with the rest of the vehicle elsewhere.

5
The Morris Minor Matures

As time went on, the image of the Morris Minor changed. The youth market looked elsewhere for more trendy designs. It would often be compared with the Mini simply because the two cars came from the imagination of the same designer, even though they were never in direct competition. Nevertheless, the Mini's arrival did lead to one very important consequence for the entire small car market. Rival manufacturers were more impressed with its performance than its size, which resulted in a move away from rear-wheel drive. By the 1970s front-wheel drive 'superminis', with a larger wheelbase than the BMC version, were being sold by major manufacturers in both the UK and Europe. Shortly before he left Morris Motors in 1952, Issigonis had experimented with a front-wheel drive Morris Minor, but the idea of a production version was never pursued.

Despite their failure to make any significant changes which would have enabled the Morris Minor to keep abreast of current trends, it continued to turn in a respectable profit, unlike some other cars in the BMC product range. In any case, personal transport went beyond the purchase of a pristine model from the showroom. Even in 1960 a new car was still an expensive commodity, requiring the support of a substantial salary. Those lower down the income scale were dependent on the thriving market in second-hand vehicles and the Morris Minor continued to be a popular choice. It had good fuel economy and was easy to maintain, making it an ideal second-hand purchase for the 'practical motorist'. It also had excellent reliability – something the sexy Mini could never boast. The saloon, convertible and traveller were beloved by the 'professional' middle classes such as doctors, district nurses, midwives and vicars. The van and pickup were popular everyday vehicles for the working man and woman.

In 1961 the Morris Minor was still very marketable. This fashion model with her elegant clothes and gloves suggests a sophisticated car for the socialite. The car has flashing indicators under the headlights rather than trafficators.

The Morris Minor dashboard was restyled in 1954, now featuring a central speedometer (being fitted here by a young factory worker in 1961). The parcel shelf was also padded to overcome criticism of sharp edges.

In 1962 the 1100 was launched, and it was this car rather than the Mini that would compete directly with the Morris Minor. These are Morris 1100s at the end of the production line at Cowley in 1966.

As time went on, the Traveller became one of the best-selling versions of the Minor and the 1,098cc engine increased its practical appeal.

In 1962 another 'advanced technology' car from the Issigonis stable was launched and this time it most definitely was a direct competitor. The Austin/Morris 1100 would become the best-selling car in this sector of the market throughout the 1960s. It had the same external dimensions as the Morris Minor, though it was lower in height, and was therefore ideal for those who found the Mini too small and the 1800 (which came along a couple of years later) too big. Issigonis even drafted his own sales brochure using the term 'new Minor', demonstrating that this was indeed his intention when designing the 1100.

Now BMC had less incentive than ever to introduce any major upgrades. The last significant change was the installation of a 1,098cc A-series in 1962, which was more about rationalisation (in as far as BMC ever considered such things) than improving the Morris Minor. This power unit was also fitted to the Austin A40, the Austin Healey Sprite and the MG Midget, as well as the newly launched 1100. Despite fitting a larger power unit, the car was still advertised and marketed as the 'Morris Minor 1000'. One possible explanation for this is that people were used to the shortened term 'Morris 1000'. Perhaps more significant from BMC's point of view was that their policy of badge-engineering meant there was already a 'Morris 1100' on the market. Obviously they wanted the public to associate this badge with their new advanced technology car without any prospect of confusing it with its fourteen-year-old cousin.

The sensible course of action would have been to take the Minor out of production and give the 1100 a clear field. The motoring press certainly thought so. In 1963, *Small Car* published its own view in an article entitled 'Home Truths':

Not that the Minor is a slow seller; from all accounts it still moves in and out of showrooms with enough regularity to keep dealers perfectly happy. Why? BMC is obviously as much puzzled as we are...Taking things all in all we fail to see how BMC can justify keeping it

Because it was still popular, the Morris Minor was not taken out of production when the 1100 appeared, but was allowed to compete with the new model for sales. These Morris 1000s are awaiting despatch from Cowley in 1962.

much longer; in most respects, great though it may have been, the Minor is well and truly outdated now. Far better to pat it affectionately on the head and put it to sleep than have it hanging around, toothless and dribbling, taking food from the others in the kennel.

BMC saw things differently. Indeed, it would seem that there was some justification in their defiance in the face of constant sniping from the motoring press because sales figures stayed remarkably steady. A clue as to why can be found in a very instructive Reader's Survey published by *Motor Sport* in August 1962. The magazine asked for feedback on a wide range of models that all came in for their fair share of criticism, though the Mini seemed to draw particular ire. Of the cars tested, the Volkswagen or the Fiat 600 came top in most categories, with the Mini scoring well for instruments and final drive. For a car of its age, the Minor's results were creditable all across the board. The killer question, however, was 'Would you buy again?' which threw up some rather more surprising results. Again Volkswagen came top with a rating of 84.7 per cent, followed by the Fiat 600 with 80 per cent. A close third, however, was the Morris Minor with 79.6 per cent, comfortably beating the Triumph Herald and Ford Anglia 105E, and way above the Mini which scored a poor 64 per cent – and even that rating carried the qualification 'only if mechanical reliability was improved'.

It was not just the general public which continued to hold the Morris Minor in high esteem. It had been adopted quite early by a number of local police forces, particularly as transport for plain-clothes 'CID' detectives. Its big moment came in 1965 when the 'Unit Beat Panda Car' was introduced. The purpose of the Panda car, so named because of its two-tone livery (though rather illogically this was blue and white rather than black and white), was to allow

The Morris Minor 1000 became a popular choice with the police when local community patrol cars were introduced. This 1,098cc version is painted with the blue and white colours that led to nickname 'Panda' car.

the 'bobby on the beat' to patrol a larger area more effectively than on foot or by motorcycle. Because the cars were fitted with two-way radios, police officers could stay in close contact with the police station, making it easier to send them on calls, while individual officers could relay information back to the station and their colleagues. This all made for a much more co-ordinated operation than had been possible until then.

In the period between 1965 and 1969 various cars were adapted as Pandas, but the Morris Minor would become one of the most popular. There were many reasons for this. The 1100, for example, was all very well, but it had complicated engineering and was prone to rust. The Minor was simple to operate, reliable, easy to maintain and robust. This durability made it perfect for police work, and not just because of the greater risk of having an accident. The patrol car had to be available to many different drivers at a moment's notice, all of whom were likely to display different levels of skill and care, which could be punishing to a squad

Did you know?

When the Austin A35 van went out of production in 1967, BMC needed a van which they could sell through their Austin dealerships, so a rebadged version of the 6 cwt Morris Minor van was sold between 1968 and 1972. This featured not just the Austin badge, but also the 'crinkled' grille. Both models were given a heavier payload option of 8 cwt, which helped boost sales, even though it was nearing the end of its production life.

Above: The van was also a popular choice for policing. This is the Sheffield Police Dog Unit in 1966. A central partition provides each dog with its own compartment.

Below: A photoshoot at Blenheim Palace in 1965 and by now the upgrades are ones of detail. Parallel wipers have replaced the 'clap hand' versions, which had carried over from the days of the split screen.

Above: The van also remained popular with local businesses such as family butcher C. Newbold. It is 1966 and the car in the background is the bestselling Austin 1100.
Below: Unfortunately the traveller's popularity was not good news because it was so expensive to make, which drastically reduced its profitability. This rear framework is being meticulously put together at the Bodies Branch in 1966.

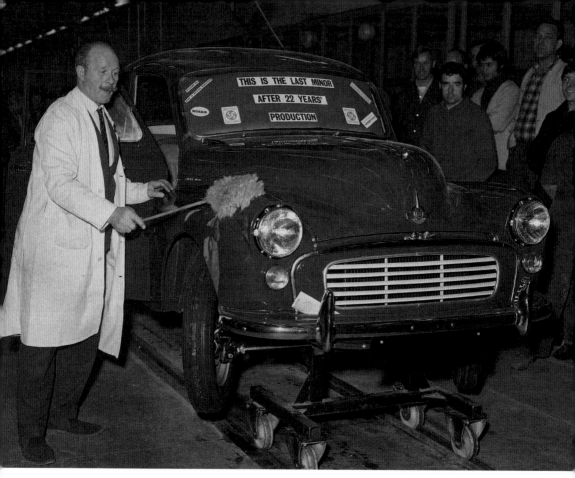

Time was finally called on the saloon in 1970. By now, the production of vans and travellers had moved to Adderley Park in Birmingham, so this was also the last Morris Minor to be built at Cowley.

car's reliability. With a top speed of 75 mph, even on the 1,098cc version, it was never going to be much use in high speed chases, but against this it was a re-assuring sight on the roads and therefore a perfect choice for 'community' policing in both town and countryside.

Then, in 1968, another merger resulted in the creation of the British Leyland Motor Corporation and suddenly the Morris Minor became the most senior model in an even bigger model range. Production techniques had moved on, and the Minor was becoming ever more expensive to manufacture meaning that the profit margin had all but disappeared. Increasingly it was the traveller that was being purchased and this was the most expensive version of all to make. So the decision was finally taken to retire it. The last convertible was made in June 1969, the last saloon in November 1970, the Traveller finished in April 1971. The commercial versions were the last to go, with the van and pickup ending production in February 1972.

Issigonis was replaced as Technical Director by Harry Webster and British Leyland wanted to take a new direction. It decided to concentrate on two new models, a conventional rear-wheel drive vehicle to compete in the fleet market and a more advanced front-wheel drive model to replace the 1100. Even though Issigonis and his designs were out of favour with the new regime, Webster readily acknowledged the merits of the Morris Minor and his original intention was to base the new fleet car on the same engineering platform. This proved impossible because the

Above: A white Morris Minor saloon was placed at the centre of the Morris section of British Leyland's Motor Show stand in 1969. It was surrounded by a cluster of younger Issigonis designs including the Mini, 1100, 1800 and Maxi.

Below: The Morris Marina quickly took the Morris Minor's place at Cowley. At the head of this production line in 1971, a 1.8 super-de-luxe coupe in flame red is being inspected as it drives off the ramp.

tooling was too worn out. Instead he developed the Morris Marina, incorporating some features carried over from the twenty-three-year-old Issigonis design.

The Morris Marina was launched in 1971 and it has been rather unfairly vilified in popular culture during the decades since it went out of production. In reality, it had a respectable if not spectacular career, selling steadily and holding its own against cars like the Ford Escort or Vauxhall Viva. Unlike the Morris Minor, however, it was the kind of affordable car that simply got you from 'a' to 'b' – neither aspirational nor ground-breaking and with little nostalgic appeal. It was therefore never going to be much-loved when it went out of production. In August 2006, *Auto Express* published a survey suggesting that only 745 of the 807,000 Marinas sold in Britain between 1971 and 1980 were still on the road, fewer than one of every thousand sold, making it, in their words 'the most-scrapped model of car sold in Britain over the previous thirty years'.

Production and sales figures do not tell the whole story when assessing the success or failure of a particular design and there is another interesting comparison that can be made between the Morris Minor, the 1100/1300, and the Morris Marina/Ital. The 1100/1300 was introduced in 1962 and total production for all models was 2.2 million over fourteen years, compared to 1.6 million over twenty-three years for the Morris Minor. The Minor's successor, the Morris Marina/Ital, was introduced in 1971 with a final total of 1.3 million over thirteen years. Then consider the fact that in 1948 only 2 million people held driving licences, in 1962 the figure was more than 10 million and by 1971 it had reached over 20 million. This shows the Minor to be by far the more successful of the three in the context of its times.

Did you know?

Actor Steve Coogan, better known as Alan Partridge, chose his fully restored Morris Minor Traveller as his luxury on *Desert Island Discs* in 2009.

6

End of Production, But Not the End

Though the advent of the Morris Marina brought with it the official end of Morris Minor production in all its forms, there was still such affection for it that it never truly became obsolete. It was no longer the stylish car with cutting-edge engineering that took the motorist's breath away at the 1948 Motor Show, but one thing it never lost was the superior handling that made it such a pleasure to drive. As car design became increasingly homogeneous and lacking in character, and the roads got ever more congested, the Morris Minor reminded its admirers of a gentler and more enjoyable period of motoring history.

It was not destined to become an aspirational supercar or a 'design icon'. Despite its popularity, it escaped the artificially inflated values that afflicted some classics. Its devotees often purchased a Morris Minor not just because they liked it, but also because they wanted to use it. A competent private owner could keep it going without too much difficulty, while more complicated work could be done by the local garage, and a supply chain quickly sprang up to feed the demand for parts. Ironically, in the longer term, Morris Minor parts would remain easy to find long after spares for more sophisticated cars such as the 1100, Allegro or Metro became more elusive. Others took advantage of its handling qualities and set about replacing the brakes, gearbox or engine to ramp up the power. There was no shortage of choices and it was not a difficult conversion to make because of the roomy engine bay, originally meant to accommodate the flat four engine. In a strange twist of fate, the car associated with district nurses and vicars in its production years now began to appeal to a younger generation. This has been a vital element in its survival because no classic car can keep going on nostalgia alone and many a club has foundered over its failure to attract a younger demographic.

1971 also marked the official retirement of Sir Alec Issigonis, though he continued to work for British Leyland as a consultant. Notable examples of each of his designs attended his retirement party, displaying their production figures to date.

Above: At the Beaulieu autojumble in 2005, the AA put on an impressive display of its preserved fleet of historic vehicles. Among them was this canary yellow Austin-badged Minor van from 1970.
Right: One of the Minor's advantages for the enthusiast is easy accessibility under the bonnet to work on the engine and ancillaries. This car is fitted with its starting handle, a feature that remained on the car until the end.

The ultimate restoration job. BMC's search for the oldest production Minor in 1961 led them to press car NWL 576. The company's apprentices faced the considerable challenge of restoring it to the pristine condition of its Monte Carlo trip.

The tangible expression of this would be the formation of the Morris Minor Owners Club (MMOC). The first official club meeting took place at Stanford Hall, Leicestershire, in April 1977, an occasion attended by twenty-seven cars with 100 members signing up. A newsletter called *Minor Matters* was established, originally as type-written foolscap sheets, which in time evolved into a lively and informative A5 glossy magazine. There was little need for formal advertising as the club soon began to attract media attention. It was featured on BBC's *Nationwide*, Thames TV's *Afternoon Plus*, and *Granada Reports*, among others. By the end of 1980, membership had risen to an impressive total of 3,550, including one Alec Issigonis who was offered, and accepted, honorary status. At that year's AGM, 400 cars arrived at Donington Park, to be joined by the first Morris Minor which was now part of the historic vehicle collection of the British Motor Industry Heritage Trust. Though Issigonis was not well enough to attend, Jack Daniels and Reg Job were among the prize-givers.

Did you know?

The Morris Minor saloon went out of production in 1970, which means the final number plates should have a 'J' suffix. In 1975, however, the Kennings dealership built a 'new' two-door Morris Minor from parts that could still be obtained through the dealership network. It was registered with an 'N' suffix number plate and can therefore claim to be the youngest Morris Minor in existence.

Aged about seven, this young car enthusiast was already fascinated by Morris Minors when his friend's grandfather offered him the treat of ride out one sunny afternoon.

Tom never lost his love of Minors. Here he is in 2014, polishing *Bluebell* to his high standards at a Concours event. He describes it as a 'process of continual improvement', gradually restoring the vehicle to its factory specification.

At the Classic Car Show in 2008, MMOC marked the 60th anniversary of the launch by recreating the 1948 Motor Show stand. They included a tableau of Issigonis' Cowley office, complete with sketches, drawing board, plan chest, and scale model.

The role of a car club can be little more than to keep a certain type of car on the road by helping to source spare parts and provide a pool of enthusiasm and knowledge. In this sense the Morris Minor had no urgent need a club since its popularity meant spare parts never became a problem and there were plenty of garages willing to help owners maintain them. This gave MMOC the opportunity to become something more, the heart of an astonishing network dedicated to 'the preservation and continued use of the post war Morris Minor'. By the fortieth anniversary of the club in 2016, the club could boast 10,000 members and sixty-four national branches, as well as being sponsor to a series of 'Registers' or special interest groups. Many of these brought together members interested in a particular model – the Series MM or Minor Million, for example. One particularly innovative section is the Young Members Register, which allows younger members to carry on their activities in a distinctive manner, yet still within the club and sharing in all its benefits.

The dedicated members of MMOC have also become famous for their imaginative displays at classic car shows both national and local, among them the Classic Car Show held at the NEC in Birmingham every November. Often adopting a themed approach, they are hard to beat when the awards for best stand are being handed out. Singing policemen with Panda cars, a mock-up village complete with shops and garages, and a recreation of the 1948 Motor

Charles Ware as a young
property developer in Bath.

Show Stand are but three stunning examples of their work. In 2002, the club was invited to take part in the closing ceremony of the Manchester Commonwealth Games, where forty-one Morris Minors, owned and driven by club members, performed a 'dance' as part of a spectacular light and sound show that was broadcast to millions of viewers all over the world.

Many Morris Minor specialists have set up businesses to support this ever growing movement. Perhaps the most remarkable was Charles Ware, the founder of the Morris Minor Centre, who developed a whole philosophy of car restoration with the Morris Minor at its heart. As a young man, Ware became a prosperous property developer in Bath. By the 1960s he was a millionaire, famous for enjoying the party life to such an extent that the *News of the World* nicknamed him 'Champagne Charlie'. At the same time, he was well-known for his social conscience and he battled to save many historic local buildings from the threat of demolition. All of this came to a sudden end when the property market crashed and he was declared bankrupt in 1975.

He was not a man to accept defeat easily, so he borrowed £200 and began to visit car auctions as a way of rebuilding his cash reserves. As he did so, he began to see a parallel between the Morris Minor and the Georgian houses that he used to buy and sell. Both, he believed were being discarded too hastily when they had great restoration potential. This gave him the idea to set up the Morris Minor Centre, which began life under a railway arch in Bath in 1976. For many years the only marketing he undertook was a fortnightly advertisement in *Exchange and Mart*, along with press publicity, which he still had a knack for attracting.

As time went on Charles Ware became more than just a garage owner, he became interested in the role of the car in society. In 1982 he published: 'Durable Car Ownership: a new approach to low cost motoring' in which he contrasted attitudes to property as a long term investment with the treatment of cars as a 'consumer durable', designed to fall apart in a few years. In his view, there was a better way. 'Treat the car like a house, like a long-term investment,' he wrote 'and there's no reason why it can't last forty years'. He expanded on this analogy:

> Any sensible householder knows that to hang wallpaper over dry rot or rising damp would be a complete waste of time and money. The motor trade on the other hand practices 'wallpapering' all the time... This means that nearly all cars are merely 'tarted up' on their downward journey to the scrapyard, even when they are in fact durables worthy of conservation.

Above: Charles Ware with some of his cars after establishing the first Morris Minor Centre. He became one of the most influential figures of the restoration movement during its early years.

Left: Cubans are experts at keeping ancient cars running. The split windscreen and bonnet (still carrying the Morris badge) show this car started life as a Morris Minor. Among its 'replacement' parts are a Lada front grille and bumper.

He cited the Morris Minor as the perfect example of the durable car. Its mechanical simplicity meant that it lacked the built-in obsolescence of modern vehicles. There was nothing that could not be replaced, repaired, or even upgraded to accommodate modern luxuries such as comfortable reclining seats and better brakes. The restoration techniques applied at the Morris Minor Centre required a complete overhaul of the car from the underframe outwards rather than the superficial 'tarting up' he criticised, and as a result it was not cheap. But his argument was that it was more economical, for the owner and for the planet, to preserve a 'durable' car than to participate in the throw-away culture fostered by the modern motor industry.

His ideas were in tune with the growing environmental awareness of the times. A contemporary movement was embodied in another book, *Small is Beautiful: A Study of Economics As If People Mattered*, written by E. F. Schumacher in 1973. This talked about the urgent need for the world to wake up to the need for sustainable development and the appropriate use of finite resources. Ware was ahead of his time in applying similar ideas to the world of classic cars. In 1991 he went into partnership with Dhanapala Samarasekara, a Sri Lankan who during his long career had been an international diplomat, a tea-planter, and a Buddhist scholar. Their shared belief in sustainable development led to the

In pursuit of his philosophy of the 'Durable Car', Charles Ware went into partnership with Dhanapala Samarasekara in 1991, setting up a factory in Sri Lanka that manufactured parts for Morris Minors.

In 2017 at the Restoration Show, the MMOC theme was the Wild West. A star exhibit was the last Morris Minor, which is roped to a fence in a makeshift corral.

setting-up of the Durable Car Company in a district of Sri Lanka that suffered from high unemployment. The factory only made parts for Morris Minors, on the basis that it was cost-effective and 'green'.

In December 2016, the Morris Minor was voted 'Britain's favourite classic car' in a poll of *Practical Classics* readers, beating the Jaguar E-type and Mini into second and third place. The judges expressed no surprise about the verdict: 'It is the classic that can never be beaten. Twelve years after we last asked you to name your favourite classic car, the Morris Minor is still on top. A British institution with a downhill parp from the exhaust evoking fond memories of days gone by ...'

Did you know?

A Morris Minor featured as part of the opening ceremony of the 2000 Olympic Games in Sydney, Australia.

7
What Now?

If you have been inspired by the story of the Morris Minor, there is an active and welcoming movement with a great support network waiting for you to join.

Clubs and organisations

Morris Minor Owners Club (MMOC), Derby, DE23 8ZX
A welcoming group with a network of regional clubs and special interest groups. Membership includes an informative newsletter *Minor Matters* and lots of benefits such as deals on breakdown services and car insurance. Their excellent website mmoc.org.uk will tell you all you need to know.

Morris Minor Centre, Bristol, BS4 5PS
The Morris Minor Centre, founded by Charles Ware, moved to Bristol in 2007 and continues to be run as a family business. As well as describing the services they offer, their website morrisminor.org.uk contains information about the history of the Morris Minor and its founder Charles Ware. It offers a number of interesting books and videos as free downloads.

Pristine Morris Minors attend a Concours event held by the Morris Minor Owners Club in 2014.

Further Reading

Bardsley, Gillian, *Issigonis, The Official Biography* (Icon Books, 2005)
McKellar, Richard and Newell, Ray, *Morris Minor 'One in a Million'* (Richard McKellar, 2010)
Moss, Pat, *The Story So Far* (William Kimber and Co., 1967)
Newell, Ray, *Morris Minor, the Complete Story* (Crowood, 1998)
Newell, Ray, *Morris Minor Owners Club, Celebrating 40 Years* (MMOC, 2016)
Overy, R. J., *William Morris Viscount Nuffield* (Europa, 1976)
Pender, Karen, *The Secret Life of the Morris Minor* (Veloce, 1995)
Skilleter, Paul, *Morris Minor, The World's Supreme Small Car* (Osprey, 1989, 3rd edition)
Thomas, Miles, *Out on a Wing, an Autobiography* (Michael Joseph,1964)
Wainwright, Martin, *Morris Minor, the Biography* (Aurum, 2008)
Ware, Charles, *Durable Car Ownership* (Morris Minor Centre, 1982, available as a download from mmoc.org.uk)

Places to Visit

The British Motor Museum (Gaydon, Warwick, CV35 0BJ) britishmotormuseum.co.uk
Housing the historic vehicle collection of the British Motor Industry Heritage Trust, including landmark vehicles such as:
Morris Minor 'Number One', 1948 (NWL 576)
Morris Minor Series II fire engine, 1953 (TFC 953)
Morris Minor 1000 Convertible, 1960 (627 BAB)
Morris Minor 1000 GPO van, 1968 (SLP 399F)

The National Motor Museum (Beaulieu, Brockenhurst, Hampshire, SO42 7ZN) beaulieu.co.uk
The historic vehicle collection includes an early Morris Minor (1949) and a late Morris Traveller (1970). Beaulieu also hosts a spring and autumn autojumble every year, an excellent place to find books, sales brochures and models relating to all types of classic vehicles.

Nuffield Place (National Trust, Huntercombe, Oxfordshire, RG9 5RY) nationaltrust.org.uk
Former home of Lord and Lady Nuffield, kept as it was when they lived there.

Morris Minor Number One, NWL 576, restored to its original condition and on display at the British Motor Museum in 2017.

A scene from the Morris Minor promotional film *Dusty Miles*. The driver contemplates a sign marking 'Contact Creek', where US Army road engineers working from the north and the south finally met in September 1942 while constructing the Alaskan Highway.

Photo and Film
A selection of historic photographs from the archives of the British Motor Industry Heritage Trust can be found on motorgraphs.com.

A DVD *The Best of Morris Minor* (HMFDVD5015) is available from motorfilms.com. This includes promotional films from the 1950s such as *Dusty Miles*, which records the Alaska Highway expedition, and *10,000 Miles Non-Stop* about the Goodwood durability trial, both of which are described in Chapter 3.

Film and TV
The Morris Minor has played a leading role in popular culture over many years, as a trawl through the authoritative IMDB database shows. Though it never received the *Italian Job* or *Bourne Identity* treatment like the Mini, it was a recurring feature of more everyday representations of life in the 1960s and 1970s. It made regular appearances in comedy programmes such as *Some Mothers Do 'Ave 'Em* and *Open All Hours*. Agatha Christie's elderly lady detective *Miss Marple* drove one, as did the rather more dashing conman and antiques dealer *Lovejoy*. Nor can we forget Roy and Hayley Cropper of *Coronation Street* who owned a 1963 Morris Minor Traveller in the soap for 12 years. ITV sold the car in 2014 after Hayley's sad demise. It was also chosen as one of the cars for Richard Wilson to drive in the series *Britain's Best Drives*. The routes chosen were all recommended by scenic guidebooks of the 1950s.

The Morris Minor puts in an appearance in all the following programmes and films which can be found on DVD, through downloading services or on YouTube:

Some Mothers Do 'Ave 'Em (BBC, 1973-1978)
Open All Hours (BBC, 1976-1985)
Agatha Christie's Miss Marple (BBC, 1984-1992)
Lovejoy (BBC, Tamariska Productions & WitzEnd Productions, 1986-1994)
Heartbeat (ITV Studios, 1992-2010)
Our Man in Havana (Kingsmead Productions, 1959)
Cul-de-Sac (Compton Films & Tekli British Productions, 1966)
Thunderball (Eon Productions, 1965)
The Borrowers (Working Title Films, 1997)
Hidden Houses of Wales (BBC Wales, 2010)
Britain's Best Drives (BBC & Twofour Broadcast, 2009)

Model Collecting

The Morris Minor has been a popular subject for model makers over many years. A wide range of choice is available, from the simplest representations costing a few pounds, to beautifully crafted items that will cost considerably more. In 1953, for example, the Nuffield Organisation and Victory Industries collaborated to produce a one-eighteenth scale replica in honour of the Coronation of Queen Elizabeth. Every detail was carefully reproduced, and it featured an electric motor that was tested under power before the body was fitted, as well as genuine Dunlop tyres.

There are too many specific models to list, but a visit to any autojumble or an internet search will turn up items from all the major model makers. At the cheaper end are Matchbox, Lledo, Vanguard and Oxford Diecast. At the top end, Victory, Pathfinder and Spot On.

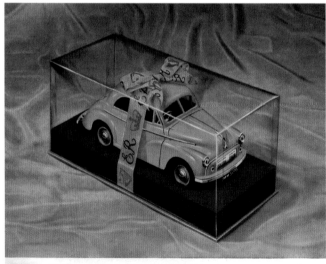

THE WORLD'S SUPREME MODEL CAR
MODELLED BY VICTORY INDUSTRIES (SURREY) LIMITED
IN COLLABORATION WITH *THE NUFFIELD ORGANIZATION*

In 1953 the Nuffield Organisation and Victory Industries crafted a one-eighteenth scale replica in honour of the Coronation of Queen Elizabeth. It was reproduced carefully in every detail and was true to scale.